GAS

KIM THOMPSON

A Crabtree Roots Book

Crabtree Publishing
crabtreebooks.com

School-to-Home Support for Caregivers and Teachers

This book helps children grow by letting them practice reading. Here are a few guiding questions to help the reader with building his or her comprehension skills. Possible answers appear here in red.

Before Reading:
- What do I think this book is about?
  - *I think this book is about balloons.*
  - *I think this book is about things that float.*

- What do I want to learn about this topic?
  - *I want to learn what gas means. Is it the same as gas you put in a car?*
  - *I want to learn how to tell the difference between a gas and something else.*

During Reading:
- I wonder why...
  - *I wonder how many things around me are gases.*
  - *I wonder what other kinds of matter there can be.*

- What have I learned so far?
  - *I have learned that gases spread out.*
  - *I have learned that air is a gas.*

After Reading:
- What details did I learn about this topic?
  - *I have learned that gas has weight even though I can't see it.*
  - *I have learned that gases have no shape.*

- Read the book again and look for the vocabulary words.
  - *I see the word **matter** on page 3 and the word **gas** on page 4. The other vocabulary words are found on page 14.*

All things are **matter**.

helium

Some matter is **gas**.

air

smoke

A gas has **weight**.

A gas is **shapeless**.

A gas **spreads** out.

Water **vapor** is a gas.

Is water always a gas?
How could you change it?

13

Word List
Sight Words

a	out
all	some
are	things
has	water
is	

Words to Know

gas

matter

shapeless

spreads

vapor

weight

All things are **matter**.

Some matter is **gas**.

A gas has **weight**.

A gas is **shapeless**.

A gas **spreads** out.

Water **vapor** is a gas.

GAS

Written by: Kim Thompson

Designed by: Rhea Wallace

Series Development: James Earley

Proofreader: Kathy Middleton

Educational Consultant: Marie Lemke M.Ed.

Photographs:
Shutterstock: Oleg Doroshin: cover; Boute: p. 1; Lopdo:
p. 3, 4-5; Eastimages: p. 7; showcake: p. 9; David
Tadevosian: p. 11; Pakhny Ushchy: p. 13

Crabtree Publishing

crabtreebooks.com   800-387-7650

Copyright © 2024 Crabtree Publishing

Printed in Canada/112023/20231130

Published in Canada
Crabtree Publishing
616 Welland Ave.
St. Catharines, Ontario
L2M 5V6

Published in the United States
Crabtree Publishing
347 Fifth Ave
Suite 1402-145
New York, NY 10016

Library and Archives Canada Cataloguing in Publication
Available at Library and Archives Canada

Library of Congress Cataloging-in-Publication Data
Available at the Library of Congress

Hardcover: 978-1-0398-0965-9
Paperback: 978-1-0398-1018-1
Ebook (pdf): 978-1-0398-1124-9
Epub: 978-1-0398-1071-6